Can Do

A collection of inspirational quotes for
teens and young adults

by ID Offokansi

Can Do

A collection of inspirational quotes for teens and young adults.

ID OFFOKANSI

978 0 9568274 0 1

Published in England by

Okid Publishing

Can Do Motivation Limited
Suite LP23783
Lower Ground Floor 145-157 St John Street
London EC1V 4PY
United Kingdom

All scripture quotations are taken from the Kings James Version of the Bible,except stated otherwise.

Yes you Can Do!

Can Do is a collection of thought provoking quotes guaranteed to spark an internal revolution in you.

This powerful book will inspire a life changing, can do attitude that will cause you to strive to be all you can be.

Targeted at youths, but very relevant to all ages and hence a book for life. These quotes have motivated me and still trigger fresh zeal for life every time I read them.

Self doubt will fade away and you will soar with a renewed can do attitude.

ID Offokansi

The heights of great men reached and kept, were not attained by sudden flight, but they, while their companions slept, were toiling upwards in the night.

Winston Churchill

Hard work always pays off;
mere talk puts no bread on
the table.

Proverbs 14:23

The Message Bible

It has been my
observation that
most people get
ahead during the
time that others waste.

Henry Ford

... And the trouble is,
if you don't risk
anything, you risk
even more.

Erica Jong

Nothing is particularly hard if you divide it into small jobs.

Henry Ford

I have not failed. I've just found 10,000 ways that don't work.

Thomas A. Edison

Nothing will work
unless you do.

Maya Angelou

There is no
substitute for
hard work.

Thomas A. Edison

Don't let what
you cannot do
interfere with
what you can do.

John Wooden

I always knew I was going to be rich. I don't think I ever doubted it for a minute.

Warren Buffett

If you do not believe
you can do it
then, you have no chance
at all.

Arsene Wenger

If you think
you can ...
... you can.

Anonymous

Before anything else,
preparation is the
key to success.

Alexander Graham Bell

People often say that motivation doesn't last. Well, neither does bathing - that's why we recommend it daily.

Zig Ziglar

Excellence is the best deterrent to racism or sexism.

Oprah Winfrey

Lost time
is never
found again.

Benjamin Franklin

Whatever you are, be a good one.

Abraham Lincoln

Positive thinking will let
you do everything better
than negative thinking
will.

Zig Ziglar

Things do not happen.
Things are made to happen.

John F. Kennedy

The toughest thing about
success is that
you've got to
keep on being a success.

Irving Berlin

If one advances
confidently in the direction
of his dreams, and
endeavors to live the life
which he has imagined, he
will meet with success
unexpected in common
hours.

Henry David Thoreau

We all have dreams. But in order to make dreams come into reality, it takes an awful lot of determination, dedication, self-discipline, and effort.

Jesse Owens

Excellence
is not a skill. It is an
attitude.

Ralph Marsto

No one gives you a break-
You create breaks, you go
out there and wrestle breaks
to the ground and beat
them into submission, you
lure them out of their caves
with sweets on a stick, you
track them down and hunt
them with an opportunity
gun, you stay in their face
until they give in - but no
one gives them away.

Richard Templar

The man who has no
imagination
has no wings.

Muhammad Ali

When you win, nothing hurts.

Joe Namath

Don't be put off by failure. Work really hard to make your idea succeed. If it doesn't, bow out gracefully and try again.

Richard Branson

If you don't practice
you don't deserve to win.

Andre Agassi

If you're walking down the right path and you're willing to keep walking, eventually you'll make progress.

Barack Obama

Dare to dream

Anonymous

I have a dream

Martin Luther King, Jr.

Everything starts with yourself, with you making up your mind about what you're going to do with your life. I tell kids that it's a cruel world, and that the world will bend them either left or right, and it's up to them to decide which way to bend.

Tony Dorsett

Action
is the foundational
key to all success.

Pablo Picasso

Faith is
taking the first step even
when you don't see the
whole staircase.

Martin Luther King, Jr.

Defeat is not the
worst of failures.
Not to have tried
is the true failure.

George Edward Woodberry

It's a funny thing
about life;
if you refuse to accept
anything but the best, you
very often get it.

W. Somerset Maugham

When written in Chinese,
the word "crisis" is
composed of two characters.
One represents danger and
the other represents
opportunity.

John F. Kennedy

Television is not real life.
In real life people actually
have to leave the coffee shop
and go to jobs.

Bill Gates

The secret of getting ahead is getting started. The secret of getting started is breaking your complex overwhelming tasks into small manageable tasks, and then starting on the first one.

Mark Twain

It's better to hang out with people better than you. Pick out associates whose behavior is better than yours and you'll drift in that direction.

Warren Buffet

Become wise by walking
with the wise; hang out with
fools and watch your life
fall to pieces

Proverbs 13:20

The Message Bible

If you want to be a winner,
hang around with winners.

Christopher D. Furman

It's fine to celebrate success
but it is more important to
heed the lessons of failure.

Bill Gates

Go as far as you can see,
and when you get there,
you will see
farther.

Anonymous

Anyone who stops learning is old, whether at twenty or eighty. Anyone who keeps learning stays young. The greatest thing in life is to keep your mind young.

Henry Ford

Failure is simply the
opportunity to begin again,
this time,
more intelligently.

Henry Ford

Nobody made a bigger mistake than he who did nothing because he could only do a little.

Edmund Burke

I don't think of myself as a poor deprived ghetto girl who made good. I think of myself as somebody who from an early age knew I was responsible for myself, and I had to make good.

Oprah Winfrey

I have fought a good fight,
I have finished my course,
I have kept the faith.

2 Timothy 4:7

Failure is success if we
learn from it.

Malcolm Forbes

Formula for success: rise early, work hard, strike oil.

J. Paul Getty

I don't know the key to success, but the key to failure is trying to please everybody.

Bill Cosby

If at first you don't
succeed, try, try again.
Then quit. There's no point
in being a damn fool about
it.

W.C.Fields

In order to succeed you
must fail, so that you
know what not to do the
next time.

Anthony J. D'Angelo

Most people give up just when they're about to achieve success. They quit on the one yard line. They give up at the last minute of the game one foot from a winning touchdown.

Ross Perot

A goal properly set is
halfway reached.

Zig Ziglar

One secret of success in life
is for a man to be ready
for his opportunity when it
comes.

Benjamin Disraeli

Success consists of going
from failure to failure
without loss of enthusiasm.

Winston Churchill

Success is simply a matter of luck. Ask any failure.

Earl Wilson

Success seems to be largely
a matter of hanging on
after others have let go.

William Feather

Success without honor is an unseasoned dish; it will satisfy your hunger, but it won't taste good.

Joe Paterno

The ladder of success is best climbed by stepping on the rungs of opportunity.

Ayn Rand

The man who has done his
level best is a success, even
though the world may write
him down a failure.

B.C. Forbes

What is success? I think it is a mixture of having a flair for the thing that you are doing; knowing that it is not enough, that you have got to have hard work and a certain sense of purpose.

Margaret Thatcher

Try not to become a man of success, but rather try to become a man of value.

Albert Einstein

All things are difficult
before they are easy.

Thomas Fuller

Everything comes to him
who hustles while he waits.

Thomas A. Edison

Never mistake activity for achievement.

John Wooden

Things may come to those who wait, but only the things left by those who hustle.

Abraham Lincoln

Hard work spotlights the character of people: some turn up their sleeves, some turn up their noses, and some don't turn up at all.

Sam Ewing

Nobody ever drowned in his own sweat.

Ann Landers

Nothing ever comes to one, that is worth having, except as a result of hard work.

Booker T. Washington

Opportunities are usually disguised as hard work, so most people don't recognize them.

Ann Lander

There is no mountain anywhere. Everyman's ignorance is his mountain.

David Oyedepo

Opportunity is missed
by most people because it
is dressed in overalls and
looks like work.

Thomas A. Edison

The only place success comes before work is in the dictionary.

Vince Lombardi

Aerodynamically, the bumble bee shouldn't be able to fly, but the bumble bee doesn't know it so it goes on flying anyway.

Mary Kay Ash

Don't limit yourself.
Many people limit them-
selves to what they think
they can do. You can go as
far as your mind lets you.
What you believe,
remember, you can achieve.

Mary Kay Ash

A winner never whines.

Paul Brown

Don't measure yourself by what you have accomplished, but by what you should have accomplished with your ability.

John Wooden

The way to get started
is to quit talking
and
begin doing.

Walt Disney

Lord, grant that I may always desire more than I can accomplish.

Michelangelo

If you don't think about
the future, you cannot have
one.

John Gale

Whether you're winning or losing, it is important to always be yourself. You can't change because of the circumstances around you.

Cotton Fitzsimmons

Don't be afraid to take time to learn. It's good to work for other people. I worked for others for 20 years. They paid me to learn.

Vera Wang

Do the one thing you think you cannot do. Fail at it. Try again. Do better the second time. The only people who never tumble are those who never mount the high wire. This is your moment. Own it.

Oprah Winfrey

To do a common thing,
uncommonly well, brings
success.

Henry John Heinz

Every choice you make has an end result.

Zig Ziglar

Sometimes we stare so long
at a door that is closing
that we see too late the one
that is open.

Alexander Graham Bell

Winning is not everything, but the effort to win is.

Zig Ziglar

About The Author

Idowu Offokansi, ID, as she is popularly known, is an IT Consultant with a deep rooted passion to help and mentor people; especially children and young adults.

She lives in London with her loving husband Okey, and their three lovely children- a boy and two girls.

She has successfully worked voluntarily with children and teenagers for charities in United Kingdom over the last ten years.

Her current endeavour i.e. this new publication - Can Do, is a reflection of some of the inspirational tools she has used to inspire a can do attitude in young people of all ages.

ID also publishes a blog (www.CanDoMotivation.com) where she publishes inspirational posters and diaries and a monthly newsletter on young people of all ages.

Visit our website,
www.CanDoMotivation.com for
our blog, motivational products and
gifts:

Books
Goal Setting Apps
T-Shirts
Stationery
Diaries
Goal Setting Journals

Notes

CPSIA information can be obtained at www.ICGtesting.com
Printed in the USA
LVOW07s0808110315

430098LV00003B/81/P